SEARCH FOR KNOWLEDGE

a collection of poems

Susan Ellis

/ BookLeaf
Publishing

India | USA | UK

Made with ❤ on the BookLeaf Publishing Platform
www.bookleafpub.in
www.bookleafpub.com

Dedication

To Don, my husband, Melissa, my radiant daughter,
To my beloved grandchildren and great-grandchildren
who are my guiding stars in this lifelong search for truth
and wonder.
To all my family and friends whose whispers echo
through my pen, and to the generations yet to come,
may this book be a lantern on your path.
In this search for knowledge, all of you are the quiet
magic, the hush between heartbeats, and the echo of
truth in the sanctuary of dreams.
This book is a tribute to the knowledge you've gifted me,
through silence, through presence, through grace.
May these poems carry forward the light you've given,
and help others find their own way.

Preface

These poems are a glimpse of my life, memory and moments. Radiating from love, loss, and wonder. Each one is a doorway shaped by family, nature and the quiet intrigue of time. I offer them with hope that you'll find your own reflection, healing, or spark within these pages.

Acknowledgements

I am grateful for my family and friends who believes in me and continues to support me through all my endives. To my beloved husband, **Don Ellis**— for your unwavering encouragement, you helped me trust the voice within. To my daughter, **Melissa Kantner**—you are the sunrise that warms every page. Your insight, grace, and gentle wisdom helped this book floursh with clarity and light. To my cherished friend, **Margie Bitetti**— Thank you for your creative spark and your unwavering encouragement. To my soul sister, **Claribel Roman**—your kindness flows like a healing stream. Your compassion and quiet strength have shaped this journey in profound ways. Without your encouragement, these words would still be dreams.

GRANDDAUGHTER'S JOURNEY

There she goes—our granddaughter, brave and bright,
Stepping through the doorway into morning light.
Not chasing dreams like her carefree peers,
But marching toward duty, shedding our tears.
Just yesterday, we cradled her small and sweet,
Now she stands tall, with purpose at her feet.
She's chosen a path of honor and grace,
To serve her country, to take her place.
We beam with pride at the strength she shows,
Armed with wisdom that steadily grows.
She'll rise through challenge, learn and strive,
With courage and heart, she'll truly thrive.
Our little girl, once soft and mild,
Now fierce and focused—still our child.
Determined, strong, she'll find her way,
And build her future, day by day.

Search for Knowledge

Oh, there was a little girl who wasn't very bright.
She was told she was stupid and would never find the
light.
She looked at all the people and politely said,
"A lot you know what's in this child's head."
Though she struggled every day, she pushed, she plowed,
she pondered her way to success.
But alas, she did not stay.
There was more to learn, more to do, more to become.
She went back to school to find the beam to help her
fulfill her dream.
She rides that lightning bolt all around town.
Who knows when she will fill her knowledge crown.

No More Scary Stories

At the party, kids told tales of
Spooky whispers, ghostly wails.
Creepy shadows, haunted halls,
Monsters creeping through the walls.
But one small child began to cry,
Tears like raindrops from the sky.
"I want my mommy," he softly said,
His cheeks were pale, his eyes were red.
The others paused, their fun now still,
A sudden hush, a silent chill.
"We're scared too," they all confessed,
Their pounding hearts beneath their vests.
So hand in hand, they formed a ring,
No more tales of goblins' sting.
They chose instead a kinder theme
Warmth and laughter, not a scream.
Popcorn popped with buttery cheer,
Its cozy scent drew smiles near.
No more frights, no ghostly gory
Just hugs and snacks, not scary stories any more.

SMILE

Smile like the sun at break of day—
Soft golden light to guide the way.
You never know whose sky you clear,
Whose storm you calm, whose heart you cheer.
A smile's a breeze through willow trees,
A hush of peace on honeyed seas.
It blooms like spring in frozen lands,
A gift of grace from gentle hands.
So smile, dear soul, and let it grow—
Like rivers dancing as they flow.
The world leans closer when you shine...
Your smile's a spark of the divine.

LOVE OF A CHILD

As a mother, I am not perfect.
I stumble. I forget.
I lose my way.
Some days, the chaos gets the best of me.
I raise my voice. I drop the ball. I feel like I'm unraveling.
But through it all
The mess, the madness, the moments of doubt
One truth remains unshaken:
No one will ever Love my child
With the fierce, boundless,
Unbreakable LOVE that I do.

WOMAN

When I hear the word WOMAN, a journey of life fills my
thoughts with:
W-warrior fighting for what is right.
O-organized keeping everything under control.
M-meaningful determined to help others understand.
A-adventuresome willing to come out of your comfort
zone.
N-nurturing, something in the wisdom of a woman's eye
can put the most troubled soul at ease.
With the eyes wide open I have discovered that beauty
and money does not make a person, but the core of one's
kindness and caring compassion is the real beauty.
When one opens their wings it changes the values of
others by flying high with chances instead of being
grounded by what ifs, that is how goals and dreams are
fulfilled.
Fill your heart and soul with
Being Brave, Being **Bold**, Being Authentic
Be **YOU**
See where the woman's journey of life takes you.

CAMPUS BUZZ

In junior high, we walked the grounds,
Girls gasped, their hearts unbound
A tanned, blonde boy with surfer stride,
Confidence he could not hide.

Their mouths agape, their feet stood still,
But I felt none of that sweet thrill.
His coolness was too much to bear,
I turned away, pretended not to care.

Then high school came, and there he was,
Golden hair, a campus buzz.
This time my mouth flew open wide,
I saw the glow he held inside.

In math class, he walked through the door,
My heart beat faster than before.
I followed him from class to class,
Behind the pillars, through the mass.

No words exchanged, just silent stares,
Until the prom, he caught me there.
A senior asking me to dance,
I said yes, seized the chance.

He spoke with kindness, calm and true,
Believed in me like no one knew.
"You can do anything," he said,
While others filled my heart with dread.

They called me slow, they called me wrong,
But he believed I could be strong.
No one expected me to shine,
But he saw something deep, divine.

I earned degrees, I found my way,
Through college halls and work each day.
Dental tools, then business plans,
Then teaching kids with gentle hands.

They remind me of the girl I was,
Who needed love, who needed trust.
Each child I meet, I learn anew,
That beauty lives in every view.

Then came my daughter, love so vast,
My heart beat loud, too full, too fast.
To raise a soul, to watch her grow,
Is love in ways I'll never know.

The surfer boy, now man and friend,
Helped me believe, helped me ascend.
We married, forty-four years strong,
His love has been my lifelong song.

From birth to now, love's shape has changed,
Through sacrifice and dreams arranged.
I find its meaning every day
In smiles, in hope, in words we say.

So if you seek where love begins,
It's in belief, not flawless skins.
It's in the eyes that see your light,
And walk beside you through the night.

I WISH

I wish I could glimpse what lies ahead
A future not blurred by sorrow's thread.
I'm weary of this endless game,
Each day I rise, each night the same.

I whisper prayers into the sky,
Begging hope to pass me by.
Is there a light beyond this haze?
A gentler path, a brighter phase?

I wear a smile like painted grace,
A mask upon my weary face.
They see the curve, the cheerful glow,
But never glimpse the ache below.

Alone I sit, the silence loud,
My thoughts a storm beneath a shroud.
Tears fall quiet, out of sight,
While others bask in borrowed light.

If they could peer beyond the grin,
They'd see the ache I hold within.
They'd feel the weight I daily bear,
And know the smile was never fair.

But still I smile, and play the part,
A fragile shield around my heart.
And those who pass, they never knew
The pain I hide, the fight I do.

WHY?

Why are we always rushing chasing time like it owes us something?
Why do the days blur, until life slips quietly by?
Why, in a blink, do we find ourselves seated,
With faded photographs and echoes, asking why?
Why didn't we pause to feel the sun on my skin?
To laugh longer, to say "I love you" more than once.
So, slow down.
Let the breeze kiss your cheek.
Let wonder find you in the ordinary.
Before the final goodbye,
Before the silence settles in, live fully
So, you never have to ask why.

JOURNEY OF LIFE

Through your journey of life,
Keep your dreams alive.
Let hope be your lantern,
And courage your guide.
When shadows grow longer,
And doubts cloud the skies,
Remember the sunrise
Still waits to arise.
Walk paths that inspire,
Climb hills that seem steep,
For treasures worth finding
Lie buried deep.
Embrace every moment,
Each joy and each tear
They shape who you are
And the life you hold dear.
So through your journey of life,
Let your spirit ignite
Keep your dreams alive,
And your heart full of light.

RAIN

The scent of rain falls soft and sweet,
A rhythm dancing at my feet.
Each puddle glimmers, none the same
A fleeting mirror, a playful game.
It washes earth in silver streams,
Cleansing dust and quiet dreams.
Peace arrives on whispered air,
A lullaby beyond compare.
Patter, patter drip and splash,
A waterfall in nature's flash.
Then silence blooms, the storm released,
A rainbow rises; all is at peace.

YES

Yes, I speak in thunder's tone,
A voice that stands, a truth full-grown.
No sugarcoat, no velvet glove—
But fierce with fire, and fierce with love.
Yes, I may seem sharp at times,
A storm that dances into rhymes.
Yet every word I choose to share
Is stitched with care, is laid out bare.
I see the world through honest eyes,
No need for masks, no sweet disguise.
My thoughts may rise like ocean spray,
But loyalty won't drift away.
So take me whole, both flame and flaw—
I'll be your shield, your steady draw.
Through every trial, near or far,
I'll be your friend—
your northern star.

FIND FRIENDS YOU CAN TOLERATE

Find a set of friends, not flawless nor grand,
But those whose quirks you gently understand.
Not perfect souls, but hearts that bend,
With faults you know, and still defend.
A laugh too loud, a stubborn streak,
A silence held when you hoped they'd speak.
Yet in their flaws, a truth you see—
A mirror of your own humanity.
Choose not the ones who never err,
But those whose faults you're glad to bear.
For love is not in faultless grace,
But in the warmth of an honest face.
So gather close your chosen few,
Whose faults are stitched in friendship true.
And thank the stars, and thank the years,
For friends who stay through joy and tears.

DANDELION

Some say you're a weed, a wild little sprite,
Popping up boldly in morning light.
Some say you're a flower, golden and sweet,
Dancing with clover beneath our feet.
Some say you're magic, a wish on the breeze,
A puff of delight that flutters with ease.
But I say you're wonder, a gift from the skies,
A sunbeam in petals, a dream in disguise.
So pluck this delight from the meadow's green bed,
Whisper your hopes to its feathery head.
Then blow with a giggle, and watch them all fly—
Your wishes like stars in the wide open sky.

RECOGNITION

I don't ask for much—
A whisper, not a spotlight.
I dwell in the shadow,
Where hidden talents bloom unseen.
Yet when others bask in praise,
And never pause to say,
"It wasn't just me—
Someone else helped shape the way,"
It stings.
Not for glory,
But for truth.
For the quiet hands
That stitched the seams
Of every shining arrangement.

ADVENTURES

Life is a journey,
We've traveled many roads,
Each adventure a lesson, Each detour a teacher.
So I say to you: never lose sight of your dreams.
Yes, the path may twist and turn, but every shift brings
new light.
This season of life is ours, A time to reimagine,
To wish boldly,
And to try something beautifully unfamiliar.
Be a little selfish.
We've nurtured children, supported partners, held
families together with grace.
Now, let's step forward. Let's stretch beyond comfort,
beyond expectation.
No more peer pressure. No more waiting.
We are women. We are strong. We are seen.
We are heard.
We are the roar in the quiet. We are the fire in the mist.
This is our time.
This is our adventure.

CRY

Keep trying, dear soul, don't let go,
The good Lord walks beside you slow.
Find your faith, let your heart lead,
In quiet strength, your spirit feeds.
He won't give more than you can bear,
His love surrounds you everywhere.
So go ahead, release the pain,
Let tears fall like gentle rain.
Each drop a prayer, each sob a song,
Each moment makes you brave and strong.
Cry, and feel the healing start,
Grace flows freely through your heart.

DOORS KEEP SLAMMING

Doors keep slamming in my face,
No open path to find my place.
Doors keep slamming, loud and fast,
I search for roots, a base to last.
Doors keep slamming, sharp and cold,
Something's chasing, fierce and bold.
Doors keep slamming, I rush, I race,
But life's not meant to be a chase.
Doors keep slamming, yet I trust
This winding road will rise from dust.
Doors keep slamming, but not in vain,
Each echo sings through loss and strain.
One day, the doors will swing wide free,
And all I've dreamed will come to be.
Desires, destiny, and grace,
Will gently guide me to my place.

Beyond the veil of everyday life lies a world woven with wonder. *Search for Knowledge* is a poetic journey through that hidden realm—a sanctuary where words shimmer like moonlight and emotions flow like ancient rivers. These verses are more than poems; they are incantations for healing, insight, and transformation. Whether you're seeking solace, clarity, or a spark of magic, you may find your spirit reflected in these pages, gently reminded of its own power to rise, dream, and remember.

Description

This collection of poetry invites you to see the world—and yourself—with fresh eyes. Each poem offers a moment of reflection, helping to soothe the soul, calm the mind, and navigate life's everyday challenges. You may find pieces of your own story woven into these verses, offering comfort, insight, and connection.

About the author

Susan is a storyteller at heart, weaving words with warmth, wonder, and a touch of charm. Her writing springs from a deep well of empathy and curiosity, shaped by quiet moments, childhood laughter, and the everyday beauty that often goes unnoticed. Whether she's crafting whimsical tales or exploring tender truths, Susan invites readers into a world where imagination and emotion walk hand in hand. She believes poetry can heal, connect, and remind us of who we are— and who we might become.